"Right," said Clive. "Let's go."

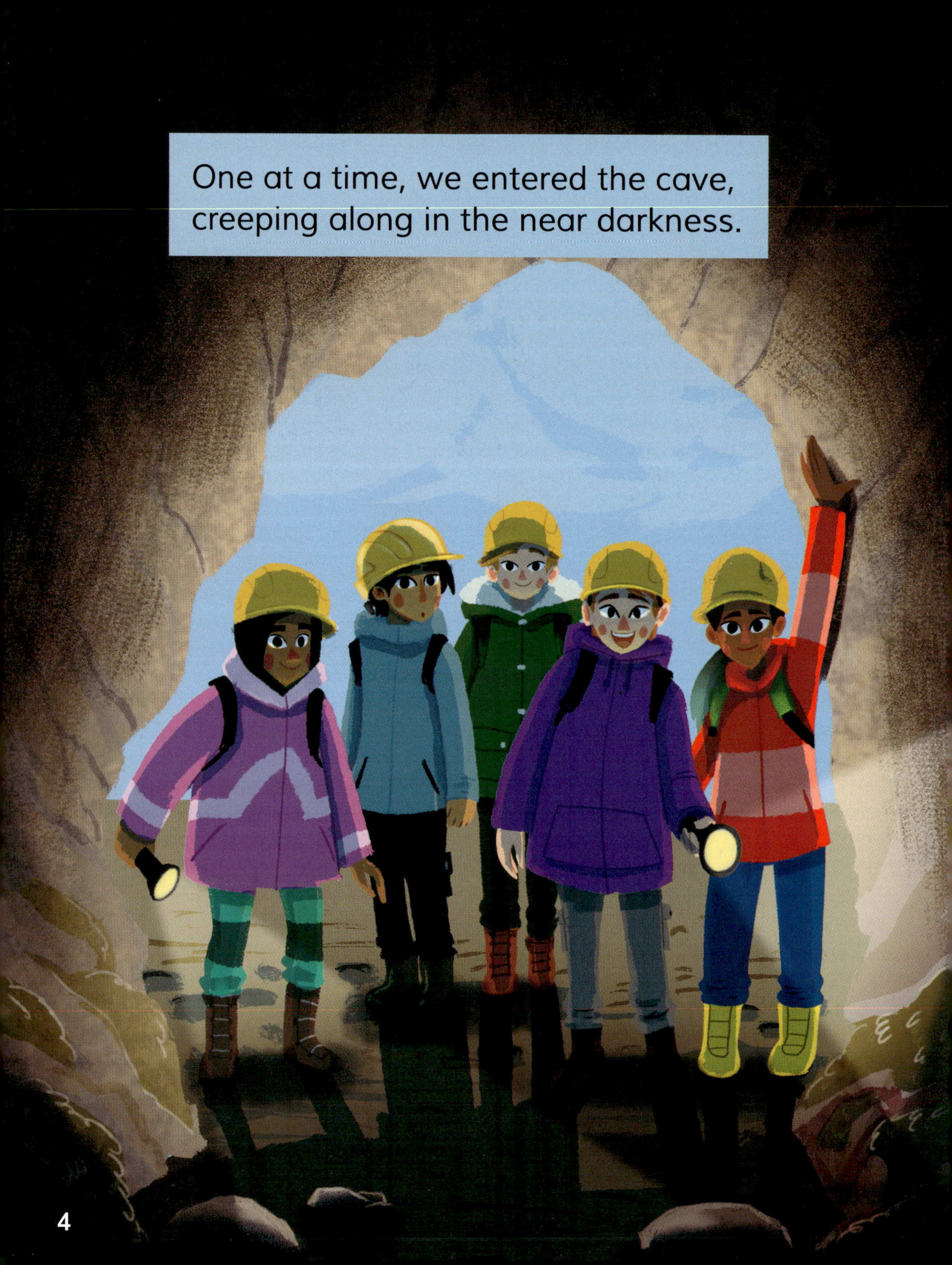

One at a time, we entered the cave, creeping along in the near darkness.

Then, all of a sudden, there was a massive crashing sound. We all felt the cave shuddering around us.

"What was that?" I asked.

Some rocks had crashed down, blocking the way out.

We were trapped in the cave!

"We have to be brave," said Clive. "No negative attitudes from now on. Let's all be positive."

Clive seemed to be the leader now. I was fine with that.

We cannot phone for help," sighed Dave. "There's no signal."

"What shall we do then?" asked Samara.

"Let's go on a bit," Clive said. "We might see a new way out."

We stopped to rest.

"I have to drink something," said Samara.

I gave her some of mine.

As I turned back, I saw a flash of red, high up.

“Look!” I shouted.

The torches lit up the cave. Hundreds of animals were painted on the rocks.

"They are stunning!" I said.

"And unexpected!" said Samara.

"How far back do you think these paintings go?" I asked.

"Maybe fifteen thousand years," said Clive. "I've seen cave paintings like this on the internet."

Then Samara spoke. "I hope we'll be rescued soon."

We had forgotten that we were still trapped underground!

We had some snacks so we didn't starve, then we kept on going.

The cave started to slope uphill, then there were loud tapping sounds.

There was a distant shout. "Are you there?"

"Yes!" Clive called. "It's good to hear you!"

The shouts grew louder.

In the end, we were rescued.

The paintings made a big splash in the news too.

Just think: if we hadn't got stuck in the cave, those paintings might never have been found!

Trends

By Daisy Hawkins

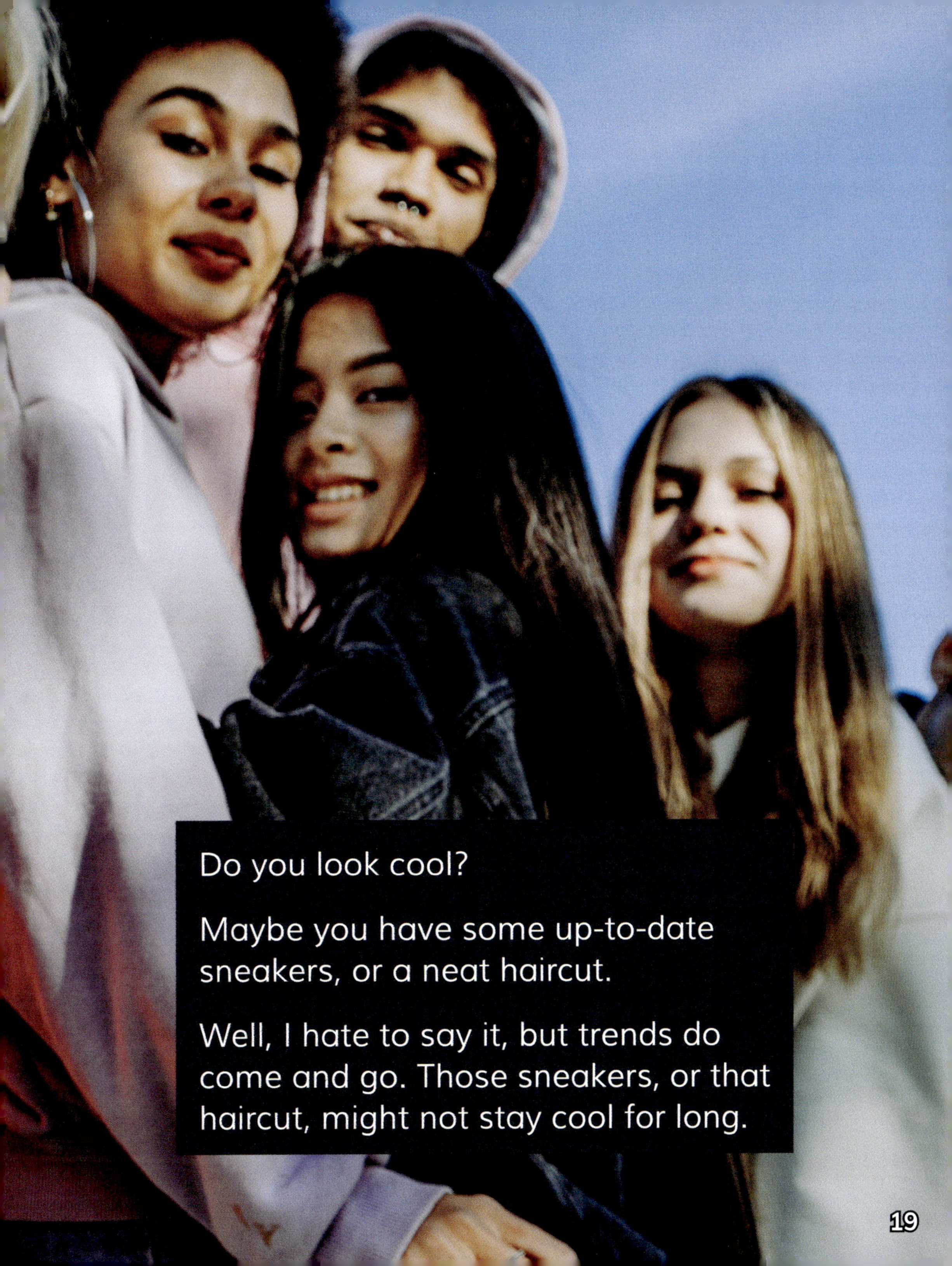

Do you look cool?

Maybe you have some up-to-date sneakers, or a neat haircut.

Well, I hate to say it, but trends do come and go. Those sneakers, or that haircut, might not stay cool for long.

Let's go back three hundred years, to when hair like this was the "in" thing.

The king of the time had thinning hair, so he looked to wigs to solve his problem.

The king set the trends, so wigs were the things to have.

Then the wigs got bigger!

As I said, trends do come and go. Do you think this trend will come back?

How about the trend of puffing up a garment with **bombast**?

Bombast was a form of stuffing made from cotton, animal hair, or even sawdust. It was like padding, to make you look bigger.

Is this a trend for the scrap heap? Or do you think it is time for it to come back?

There was a time when **hoop skirts** were the newest thing.

A frame, made of steel, whalebone, or wood, was worn under a dress to give it a bell shape.

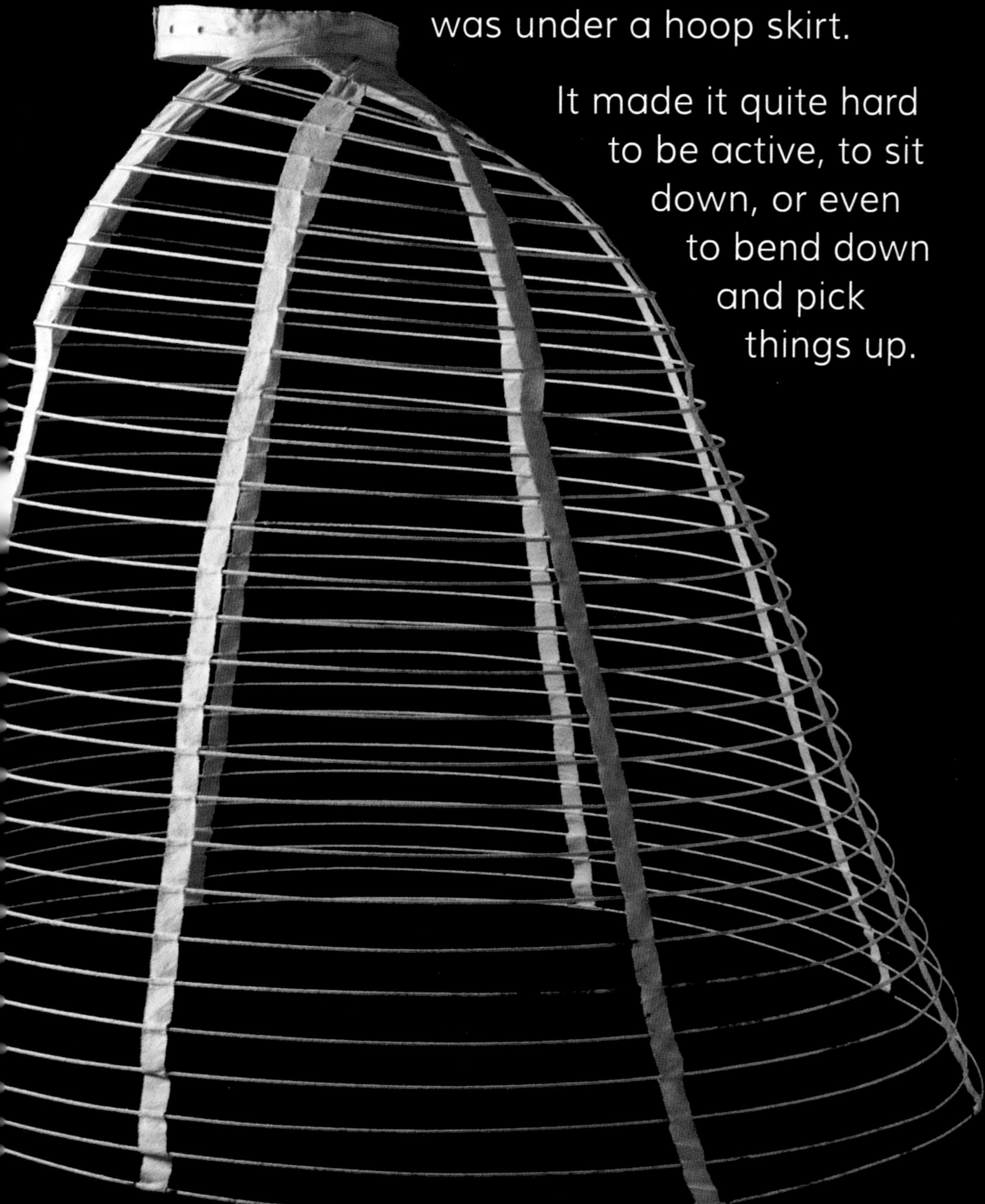

This is the sort of frame that was under a hoop skirt.

It made it quite hard to be active, to sit down, or even to bend down and pick things up.

The white thing around this man's neck is a **ruff**.

Ruffs started as a modest embellishment to an outfit.

Then, thanks to the import of starch (which helps fabric stay in shape), ruffs started to get bigger.

The extreme ones were called "cartwheel ruffs." With the help of some thin wire, they were at least a foot wide.

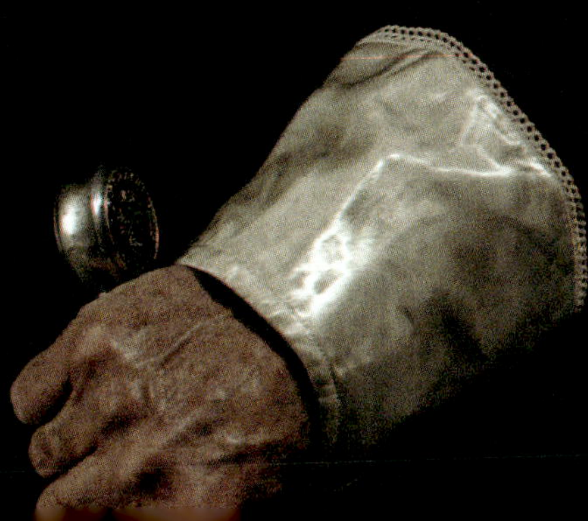

Look at the thick soles on these!

Back in the 1970s, people liked platforms like this. They were often worn with wide trousers and bright shirts.

As you can see, this look even ended up on some stamps.

This is called a **crakow**.

Crakows were all about having the longest pointed toe.

If you had these, you were rich. They were expensive – and quite impractical.

Trends come and go, and this trend has come back a few times.

Are you a fan?

So do not boast too much about how up-to-date you look right now.

Give it a few hundred years and you might end up in a book like this one!

The Monster Coach

Written by
Stephen Rickard

Illustrated by
Pablo Gallego

Jade and Dean played for the district Under-16s team. It was a good team, but training was boring.

Frank, the team coach, was too strict. They just seemed to do drills all the time. Frank's assistants, Jeff and Hunter, were just as bad.

"Frank's like a monster," Jade muttered, as she ran up and down.

"Let's have some fun," said Dean. "Let's tell the team that Frank is a monster. Some of the kids might think it's true."

So Jade and Dean did tell little Eric that Frank was indeed a monster – from a massive, distant planet.

Little Eric was shocked.

The problems started when Eric informed his teacher, Mrs. Jones.

"What?" said Mrs. Jones. "A monster? Are you positive that Jade and Dean said this?"

"Oh yes," said little Eric.

The next day, Mrs. Jones spoke to Eric's mom. Then she had a meeting with all the teachers.

The teachers all agreed that they had to solve this.

"Leave it with me," said Mrs. Jones.

In the meantime, Eric's mom had chatted with the moms of all the players in the team.

Things were getting out of hand.

Then the TV news got to hear of it.

They rang Mrs. Jones and, that night, she was on the news, saying that Frank might or might not be a monster – they were still looking into it.

On the next day, Frank was sent into a meeting with the teachers. The moms and dads of all the players were there too. Jeff went to give Frank some support.

They asked Frank if he was in fact a monster.

I do not need to tell you how the meeting went.

Frank was shocked and said, "What? No!" lots of times.

In the end, they all had to agree that Frank was not a monster.

They were quite glad in fact, as no one likes a monster from a distant planet running the district soccer team.

They all asked Frank to forgive them.

Jade and Dean got a good telling off as well.

At the next week's training, Frank spoke to all the players.

"Well, you had some fun," said Frank. "But now it's clear that I'm not a monster, let's all do some good training!"

At the end of training, the players all left, leaving just Jeff and Hunter.

“Gosh, that was close!” said Hunter, as he and Jeff peeled off their skins. “We need to be extra-attentive from now on.”